# Titanic!

Paul Shipton

Level 3

Series Editors: Andy Hopkins and Jocelyn Potter

**Pearson Education Limited**

Edinburgh Gate, Harlow,
Essex CM20 2JE, England
and Associated Companies throughout the world.

Pack ISBN: 978-1-4058-8449-5
Book ISBN: 978-1-4058-8402-0
CD-ROM ISBN: 978-1-4058-8401-3

First edition published 2001
This edition published 2008

3 5 7 9 10 8 6 4 2

Text copyright © Paul Shipton 2008

Illustrations by Francisco Solé
Illustrations for 'A Passenger's Story' copyright © Jeff Anderson
Illustrations pp. 4-5 copyright © David Cuzic
Illustrations pp. 7 and 29 copyright © Alan Fraser
Map on pp. 44-45 by Witmor

Set in 11/13pt A. Garamond

Printed in China

SWTC/02

Produced for the Publishers by AC Estudio Editorial S.L.

Published by Pearson Education Ltd in association with Penguin Books Ltd,
both companies being subsidiaries of Pearson Plc

**Acknowledgements**

We are grateful to the following for permission to reproduce photographs:
(Key: b-bottom; c-centre; l-left; r-right; t-top)
**Alamy Images:** imagebroker / Norbert Michalke page 59; **Aquarius Collection:** Paramount / 20th Century
Fox pages 28, 49t, 51t; **Corbis:** Corbis Sygma / Steve Azzara page 2bl; Corbis Sygma / Los Angeles Daily
News page 2br; Hulton-Deutsch Collection page 41; Underwood & Underwood page 42; Ralph White pages
45, 46; **Getty Images:** AFP / Hector Mata page 2t; **Ronald Grant Archive:** Paramount / 20th Century Fox
pages 16, 48; © **National Maritime Museum, London:** page 54; **The Picture Desk:** The Kobal Collection /
Paramount / 20th Century Fox pages 3, 49b, 50t, 50b, 51b, 52; **TopFoto:** Charles Walker page 1;
**www.maritimequest.com / Michael W. Pocock:** pages 5, 6, 8, 9, 36

Picture Research by Sarah Purtill

Every effort has been made to trace the copyright holders and we apologise in advance for any
unintentional omissions. We would be pleased to insert the appropriate acknowledgement
in any subsequent edition of this publication.

For a complete list of the titles available in the Penguin Active Reading series please write to your local
Pearson Longman office or to: Penguin Readers Marketing Department, Pearson Education,
Edinburgh Gate, Harlow, Essex CM20 2JE, England.

# Contents

## 1.1 What's the book about?

**How much do you already know about the _Titanic_?**

**1** In 1912, the _Titanic_ was the biggest ship ever built. How long was it?
  a 269 meters (882 feet)
  b 149 meters (489 feet)
  c 328 meters (1,076 feet)

**2** How many people died on the _Titanic_?
  a 500
  b more than 1,500
  c 250

**3** Where was the _Titanic_ traveling to?
  a Southampton
  b Nova Scotia
  c New York

**4** There were more than 2,200 people on the ship. How many people could the lifeboats carry?
  a 2,278
  b 1,178
  c 1,923

**5** How many third-class passengers died?
  a 10%
  b 25%
  c 75%

**6** Which ship picked up the people who were still alive?
  a the _Carpathia_
  b the _Olympia_
  c the _Californian_

**7** After the accident, when was the _Titanic_ seen again?
  a 1985
  b 1959
  c 1995

**8** How many Oscars did James Cameron's 1997 movie _Titanic_ win?
  a 5
  b 8
  c 11

## 1.2 What happens first?

Look at the title of Chapter 1. What dreams do you think these people had? Make notes.

| | |
|---|---|
| Rich passengers in first class | |
| Poor passengers in third class | |
| The ship's builder | |
| The ship's owners | |

# The Ship of Dreams

*The ship could carry more than 3,000 passengers,*
*but it only had lifeboats for 1,178 people.*

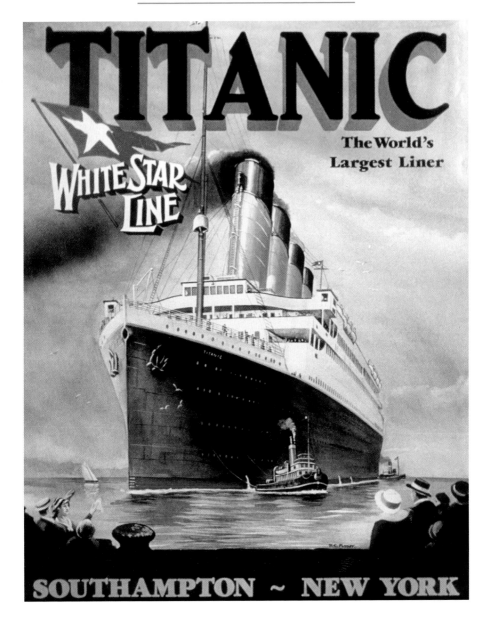

## ● The king of the world!

James Cameron was the big winner at Oscar night in Los Angeles in March 1998. His 1997 movie was named Best Picture, winning ten other Oscars, too. As Cameron held up the Oscar, he repeated a famous line from the movie: "I'm the king of the world!" He later joked that "size does matter."

It was a dream that Cameron had for a long time. He loved history and he was always interested in the story of the *Titanic*. Cameron's early movies—for example, *The Terminator* and *Aliens*—were full of action. *Titanic* had plenty of action, too, but the heart of the movie was a love story. Cameron chose two young actors for this.

Leonardo DiCaprio played Jack Dawson. Born in 1974, DiCaprio was first seen on TV at the age of five. He became famous in the 1990s with movies like *What's Eating Gilbert Grape?* and *This Boy's Life*. Work on Cameron's *Titanic* was long and difficult for DiCaprio.

Kate Winslet played Jack's lover, Rose. The British actress was also born in 1974. Winslet was not interested in small parts in Hollywood movies. She wanted to act in the theater. But soon Kate was in the biggest movie that was ever made.

While Cameron was making the movie, not everybody was so sure about its success. It took a long time to make the movie. As it continued, the cost went up and up. It finally cost between $185,000,000 and $200,000,000. The movie's opening was changed from summer of 1997 to December. Many newspapers and magazines wrote stories about the movie like " *Titanic* **Sinks**."

*Titanic* was more expensive than any other movie:

- For the first part, Cameron filmed the real *Titanic* at the bottom of the ocean. He had to go down to the ship in a **submarine** twelve times.
- Cameron filmed most of the movie on a **model** that was almost as big as the *Titanic*. He wanted everything on the ship to be like the real *Titanic*. Clothes, furniture, machines—everything had to be exactly right.

Not all newspapers and magazines liked the movie. One called it "dead in the water." But people around the world loved it. The world's most expensive movie became the biggest success. It earned over $1,600,000,000!

sink /sɪŋk/ (v) to go down below the water
submarine /ˈsʌbməˌrin, ˌsʌbməˈrin/ (n) a ship that can travel underwater
model /ˈmɑdl/ (n) a small copy of something that is going to be much bigger

**Lifeboats**

*There were twenty lifeboats on the ship.*

**Compartments**

*There were sixteen compartments on the ship.*

## The biggest and the best!

In the 1900s, more and more people wanted to travel across the Atlantic Ocean. The ships became bigger and better, as ship companies fought hard for customers. In 1907, the White Star Line decided to build the biggest and the best of all. The company planned to make three ships. Their names said a lot about them—*Olympic*, *Titanic*, and *Gigantic*.

Next to the *Titanic*, most other ships seemed small. It was 269 meters (882 feet) long. At the time, the tallest building in the world was only 229 meters (750 feet).

Everyone thought that the ship was also very safe. There were sixteen compartments. In an accident, big metal doors could close and then no water

### ● Bridge

*The ship's bridge gave the captain and officers a good view.*

### ● Decks

*The ship had nine different decks. The top one was the boat deck.*

could get from one compartment to another. The ship was even able to **float** with the first 4 compartments full of water!

The *Titanic* became the famous "unsinkable ship." Nobody seemed to worry about another important fact. The ship could carry more than 3,000 passengers, but it only had lifeboats for 1,178 people.

**float** /fləʊt/ (v) to stay on the top of the water without going under it

## ● "That ship is going to sink!"

Can some people see the future? Can dreams ever show what is going to happen? A few strange things happened before the *Titanic* sailed for the first time in 1912.

### Strange Books

- In 1898, Morgan Robertson wrote a book called *Futility*, or *The Wreck on the Titan*. The book told the story of a ship crossing the Atlantic. It hit an **iceberg** and sank. Almost all of the passengers died because there weren't enough lifeboats.
- Six years earlier, in 1892, William T. Stead wrote *From the Old World to the New*. In that story, too, a ship hit an iceberg and sank. Another ship picked up the **survivor**s. The **captain**'s name was E. J. Smith—the name of the *Titanic*'s captain. Twenty years later, Stead traveled on the real *Titanic*. He didn't survive.

### Dreams and Bad Feelings

- The Adelmans were planning to return to the United States on the *Titanic*. Suddenly, Mrs. Adelman had a terrible feeling of danger. She and her husband didn't travel on the *Titanic*.
- Mrs. Blanche Marshall watched the *Titanic* from an island near Southampton. "That ship is going to sink before it reaches America," she said. "I can see hundreds of people in the icy water."

The *Titanic* left Southampton, on the south coast of England, at noon on April 10, 1912. Even at the start of the trip, the *Titanic* had bad luck. There was almost an accident in the first minutes of the trip.

The danger passed, but for some people this was a bad start to the famous ship's first trip across the Atlantic. Some people said, "It's bad luck!"

iceberg /ˈaɪsbɜɡ/ (n) a very large piece of ice in the ocean
survive /səˈvaɪv/ (v) to continue to live after an accident or other danger
captain /ˈkæptən/ (n) the person who gives orders to sailors and other workers on a ship

**A** *The* Titanic *sailed past two other ships, the* Oceanic *and the* New York.

**B** *Because the* Titanic *was so big, the* New York *was pulled closer toward it. The ropes broke on the smaller ship. It began to float toward the* Titanic.

**C** *Luckily, a small boat was able to tie a rope onto the* New York. *It pulled the smaller ship out of the way.*

At this time of year, there was also a danger of icebergs in the North Atlantic. But the *Titanic*'s captain, Edward Smith, wasn't really worried about ice—this was the unsinkable *Titanic*!

**rope** /roup/ (n) something long, strong, and thick. It is used to tie two things together.

## ● The Queen of the Ocean

The *Titanic* was able to carry more than 3,000 people, but there were only 2,207 people on the ship for its first trip.

| | |
|---:|:---|
| First class: | 322 passengers |
| Second class: | 275 passengers |
| Third class: | 712 passengers |
| Crew: | 898 people |

The different classes didn't mix on the ship. They slept, lived, and ate on different decks. Of course, the first-class passengers were on the higher decks. The second-class passengers were in the middle. Then came the third-class passengers, at the bottom.

### *First Class*

The White Star Line called the *Titanic* "the Queen of the Ocean." For first-class passengers, life on the *Titanic* was as comfortable as life in the most expensive hotels in Europe and America. There were hundreds of **servants** to look after them. Their private rooms were large and comfortable. They could enjoy a swimming pool, a library, Turkish baths, and excellent restaurants and bars.

Some of the richest people in the world were on the ship. In fact, American John Jacob Astor IV was possibly the richest of all. In 1912 he had $87 million. (That is more than $1,500,000,000 today.)

crew /kru/ (n) the people who work together on a ship
servant /ˈsəvənt/ (n) somebody who works in another person's home

Bruce Ismay, the president of the White Star Line and Thomas Andrews, the ship's builder, were also on the *Titanic*.

### Second Class

Life for the passengers in second class was comfortable, too. In fact, second class on the *Titanic* was as nice as first-class travel on many other ships. These passengers also had a library and a few bars. They, too, could walk around on an open deck and enjoy views of the ocean.

### Third Class

More than half of the passengers were in third class. Of course, life on these decks wasn't as comfortable. But the rooms were clean and bright.

More than 100 of the third-class passengers were from Ireland. The others came from many different countries in Europe. Most of them had the same dream. They were leaving their problems in their own countries. For them, the United States of America was the promise of a new life.

# A Passenger's Story

**Part 1**

Seventeen-year-old Jack Thayer was on the Titanic after a vacation in Europe with his parents.

I don't think I'll be bored on this ship!

He used the ship's swimming pool every day.

A ship with a swimming pool!

On Sunday evening, while his parents ate dinner with the captain, Jack ate alone.

Excuse me. Can I have a light?

Of course.

The two young men talked for a long time.

This ship's wonderful, isn't it?

I was on a ship that sank once. It was near Alaska.

The man's name was Milton Long. He was traveling home to the United States, too.

I must go to my room. My parents will be worried. Good night, Milton.
See you tomorrow, Jack.
That night ...
That's strange. This ship has stopped.
What's wrong?
Something's happened. I'm going out on deck to see the fun!
I'll join in a minute, Jack.
We hit an iceberg. I'm sure of it.
An iceberg?
Continues ...

## 2.1 Were you right?

Look back at your answers to Activity 1.2. Then decide if these sentences are true (✓) or untrue (✗). Write the untrue sentences correctly below.

1 ☐ The first-class passengers could enjoy a library and a pool.
2 ☐ The third-class passengers were on the higher decks.
3 ☐ Most of the third-class passengers came from Ireland.
4 ☐ The ship's compartments were meant to make the ship safer.
5 ☐ The White Star Line put enough lifeboats on the ship for every passenger.

..................................................................................................................
..................................................................................................................
..................................................................................................................

## 2.2 What more did you learn?

Choose a name from box A and words from box B to complete each sentence below.

**A**
William T. Stead
Kate Winslet
Mrs. Adelman
James Cameron
White Star Line
Leonardo DiCaprio

**B**
the theater
the king
an iceberg
a feeling of danger
the *Titanic*
Jack Dawson

1 When he won an Oscar, .....James Cameron..... said, "I'm .....the king..... of the world!"

2 ........................ found it difficult playing third-class passenger ........................ .

3 British actress ........................ wanted to act in ........................ more than in movies.

4 The ........................ owned ........................ .

5 In an earlier book by ........................ , a ship hit ........................ .

6 ........................ refused to travel on the *Titanic* because she had ........................ .

## .3 Language in use

Look at the sentence on the right. Then complete the sentences below with superlative forms of the adjectives.

> The White Star Line decided to build the **biggest** and **best** of all.

1   In 1997 *Titanic* was the ............*biggest*............ movie of the year. (big)

2   At the time, it was the ................................. movie ever. (expensive)

3   The ................................. building in the world was 229 meters (750 feet). (tall)

4   Parts of the ship were as comfortable as the ................................. and the ................................. hotels in Europe. (good, expensive)

5   The ................................. passengers were on the higher decks. (rich)

6   ................................. of the third-class passengers were looking for a new life in the United States. (many)

## .4 What happens next?

Read the title of Chapter 2 and the lines in italics below it. Then look at the pictures in this chapter. What do you think? Make notes.

1   Why didn't the *Titanic* miss the iceberg?

2   How did the passengers feel when they first heard about the iceberg?

Notes

# Danger!

*Many passengers heard the noise, but it wasn't very loud.
Nobody knew it yet, but this was the beginning of the end for the* Titanic.

On Sunday, April 14, while the passengers enjoyed life on the *Titanic,* **radio operators** Jack Phillips and Harold Bride were busy. Many passengers wanted to send personal messages to friends and relatives on land. But Phillips and Bride were receiving messages from other ships also.

 Early in the afternoon, Phillips received an ice **warning** from a ship called the *Baltic.* It was the third warning of the day. The message was taken to the bridge, but Captain Smith didn't show it to his officers until 7:15 P.M.

It was a cold, clear evening now. Seeing the message about ice, Second Officer Lightoller told the **lookouts** to watch carefully for icebergs.

 In the radio room, Jack Phillips took another message about icebergs **ahead**. It never reached the bridge. Phillips put it down on his desk and continued with his work.

Phillips received another message. This one was from a ship called the *Californian.* The ship couldn't move through the ice. "**Shut up**, shut up," Philips said. "I'm busy."

 Lookouts Frederick Fleet and Reginald Lee were cold and tired. Suddenly, Fleet saw a large, black shape in the ocean. He rang the warning three times and telephoned the bridge.
"Iceberg right ahead," he told Sixth Officer James Moody.

**radio operator** /ˈreɪdiˌoʊ ˈɑpəˌreɪtəˈ/ (n) somebody who has the job of using the ship's *radio*
**warning** /ˈwɔrnɪŋ/ (n) something that tells people of a possible danger
**lookout** /ˈlʊk-aʊt/ (n) a person who watches carefully for danger
**ahead** /əˈhed/ (adv) in front
**shut up** /ˌʃʌt ʌp/ (v) to be quiet (used rudely)

On the bridge, First Officer William Murdoch had to act fast. He turned the ship left, hoping to miss the iceberg. He also ordered the crew to stop the ship.

The iceberg was thirty meters higher than the top decks. Some ice fell onto the deck as the ship passed it. But nothing broke. It was a different story under the water. The iceberg hit the side of the ship, making a few long holes below the water. Many passengers heard the noise, but it wasn't very loud. Nobody knew it yet, but this was the beginning of the end for the *Titanic*.

Captain Smith hurried to the bridge.

"What have we hit?" he asked Murdoch.

"An iceberg, sir," replied the First Officer.

Soon Bruce Ismay of the White Star Line was on the bridge, too. Fourth Officer Joseph Boxhall went to check the lower decks. Fifteen minutes later, he reported, "Water is coming in."

Captain Smith and the ship's builder, Thomas Andrews, went below to check. Andrews immediately understood the terrible danger. The ship could float with water in the four compartments at the front, but there was water in five of the compartments. There was no hope. The *Titanic* was sinking.

 There was only one thing that Captain Smith could do now. Just after midnight, he ordered the crew to prepare the lifeboats.

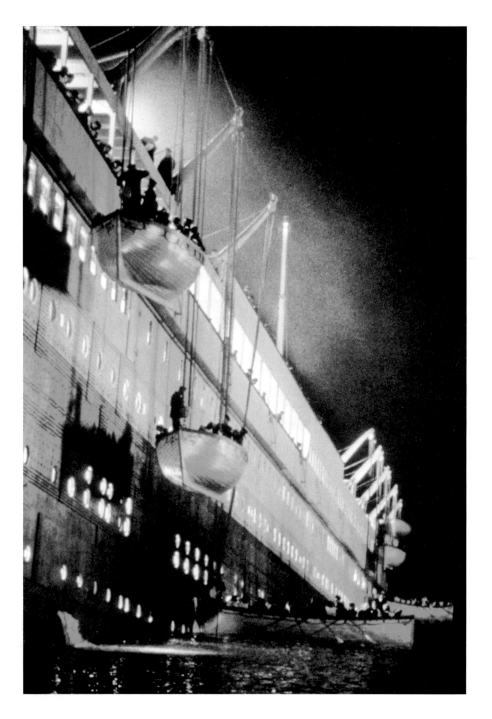

## ● "Women and children first"

After Smith gave the order, the crew started to wake the passengers. They told them to put on their life jackets and warm clothes. Passengers should go to the boat deck.

At first, many of them didn't believe the danger—of course, the *Titanic* couldn't sink! Some of the first lifeboats were almost empty. There were twelve people in one boat for seventy people.

As the front end of the *Titanic* sank lower and lower in the water, more passengers began to understand the danger. But they still didn't know the most terrible fact of all. There were more than 2,200 people on the *Titanic*, but the ship had lifeboats for only 1,178!

Parents said goodbye to their children. Husbands kissed their wives for the last time. One woman's husband told her, "You go. I will stay." The lifeboat left, and she never saw him again.

- First-class passenger Molly Brown was put into the third lifeboat and she helped to get the boat away from the ship. Later, she saved a dying man, keeping him warm with her coat.
- An old woman, Mrs. Ida Straus, decided not to go into a lifeboat. She couldn't leave her husband. "We have lived together and we will die together," she said.
- One man put on women's clothes and tried to get into a lifeboat. The officer sent him away angrily.
- Third-class passenger Minnie Coutts didn't have enough life jackets for her two sons. One of the crew gave his life jacket to her. "There!" he said. "If the boat goes down, you'll remember me!"

By one o'clock, the danger was clear to everybody. Now there was no problem filling up the boats and the officers had a different problem. They had to keep people away. Guns were given to the officers on the boat deck.

## ● "Come Quick!"

While the crew began to fill the lifeboats, radio operators Jack Phillips and Harold Bride began to send messages for help. Their message was CQD— "Come quick, danger."

At first Phillips and Bride weren't worried. They even made jokes as they worked.

"You'll see your first iceberg," said Phillips with a laugh.

"The Americans will enjoy it," answered Bride. "They all like to have ice in their drinks."

The first replies came from ships that were too far away. Then Phillips heard from the *Carpathia*. The ship was traveling from New York to the Mediterranean. The *Carpathia's* radio operator, Cyril Evans, couldn't hide his surprise. He immediately told Arthur Rostron, the captain of the *Carpathia*.

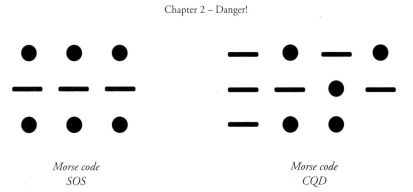

Morse code
SOS

Morse code
CQD

Then he called the *Titanic* again. The Carpathia was turning around. It was coming to help. But there was a problem. The *Carpathia* was about ninety-three kilometers (58 miles) away. It could reach the *Titanic* in four hours. That was too long—the *Titanic* had less than two hours.

Now Phillips and Bride understood the danger. They continued to send messages, hoping to find a closer ship. The *Titanic* was becoming noisier and their job became harder and harder.

As they worked, Phillips and Bride started sending the new help message, SOS. The *Titanic* was the first ship that sent an SOS message. It was quicker and easier to send.

The two men bravely stayed in the room until it was almost the end. Their last message was sent at 2:17 A.M. Outside on the deck, hope was growing. Captain Smith and Fourth Officer Boxhall could see the lights of a ship that was only 9.5–16 kilometers (6–10 miles) away. The crew tried to send a message to the ship with a light. Then, at 12:45 A.M., they began to send **rockets** high into the dark sky. They sent a rocket every five minutes. At first, the ship seemed to be coming closer. But then its lights disappeared. Hopes of help for the *Titanic* disappeared with them.

What was the ship that was so close? Why didn't it help?

- Some people think that it was the *Californian*. In fact, the crew of the *Californian* did see lights in the sky and the lights of a ship. But the ship seemed quite small to them. When they tried to send a message to it, there was no answer.
- Did the officers on the *Titanic* see a different ship? More and more people today think that it was a Norwegian fishing boat. Why didn't it help? Maybe it was breaking the law by being in the area.

**rocket** /ˈrɑkɪt/ (n) a bright light that is sent up from a ship. It is a sign that a ship is in trouble.

# A Passenger's Story

## Part 2

Activities 3

## 3.1 Were you right?

**Look back at your answers to Activity 2.4. Then circle the correct answers below.**

1  On the evening of April 14, it was ...
   **a**  cold and clear.    **b**  warm.    **c**  very windy.
2  When the iceberg hit the ship, there was ...
   **a**  a very loud noise.    **b**  a little noise.    **c**  no noise.
3  When the crew woke them, at first many passengers ...
   **a**  were very afraid.    **b**  did not understand.    **c**  were angry.
4  Passengers began to believe the danger when ...
   **a**  the captain explained.  **b**  lifeboats were lowered.
   **c**  the front of the ship sank.

## 3.2 What more did you learn?

**Many mistakes were made on the *Titanic*. Put these in the right order. Number them, 1–9.**

**a**  ☐  The First Officer turned the *Titanic* left hoping to miss the iceberg.

**b**  ☐  Phillip told the radio operator from the *Californian* to be quiet.

**c**  1  The radio operators were sending messages for passengers when ice warnings arrived.

**d**  ☐  Second Officer Lightoller told the lookouts to watch carefully for icebergs.

**e**  ☐  The captain didn't show the warning to his officers immediately.

**f**  ☐  The lookouts saw the iceberg right ahead of the ship.

**g**  ☐  The iceberg made long holes in the ship below the water.

**h**  ☐  Captain Smith ordered the crew to prepare the lifeboats.

**i**  ☐  The captain and the builder checked the compartments.

## 3.3 Language in use

**Look at the sentences on the right. Then complete these sentences with passive verb forms.**

> The message **was taken** to the bridge.
>
> Molly Brown **was put** into the third lifeboat.

1 An ice warning from another ship ............................... in the afternoon. (receive)

2 A few long holes ............................... in the ship below the water. (make)

3 Passengers ............................... to go to the boat deck. (tell)

4 One man in women's clothes ............................... away from the lifeboats. (send)

5 The lights of another ship ............................... not far away. (see)

6 The last lifeboats ............................... quickly. (fill)

## 3.4 What happens next?

**Look at the pictures on pages 24–27. Do you think these statements are true (✓) or untrue (✗)?**

1 ☐ Many third-class passengers could not reach the boat deck.

2 ☐ Everybody fought to get into the lifeboats.

3 ☐ All the lifeboats were completely full.

4 ☐ Some passengers were getting ready to die.

5 ☐ The ship broke in two pieces.

6 ☐ The crew had to use a gun to keep order.

7 ☐ The band played until the lights went off.

# CHAPTER 3

# The Sinking Ship

*Suddenly, the front of the ship moved more quickly down into the water.*
*A big wave began to move up the boat deck.*

● **"Well, boys, do your best!"**

After one o'clock on the morning of April 15, the *Titanic*'s front end was sinking fast. The band still played and the lights were on. But everyone knew what was happening. And there were few lifeboats left.

- A fourteen- or fifteen-year-old boy tried to hide on a lifeboat. The ship's officer pointed a gun at him. "Be a man," he said. The boy left the lifeboat.

- When one lifeboat hit the water, its ropes were still joined to the ship. Before it could get away, another lifeboat began to come down on top of it. Luckily, a crewman cut the ropes with a knife in time.

## ● Was it true?

Many people believe that the third-class passengers were kept away from the boat decks. It is true that many of these passengers lost their lives.

Some of the crew did try to help the third-class passengers to the boats. The job wasn't easy. Passengers had to go up the ship's many decks. Many of them didn't speak English. They didn't understand the danger. Some refused to follow the crew and stayed on their deck.

Some doors were locked by the crew. Nobody really knows why. Were they following orders? Were they just afraid? But women and children from third class *were* sent to the boat deck. The most crowded lifeboat left at 1:25 A.M. with seventy people in it. Most of them were women and children from third class. But the men were still kept away from the boat deck. When they reached it at last, it was too late. Almost all the lifeboats were gone.

By two o'clock, the water was just below the boat deck. When the crew were preparing the next lifeboat, a crowd tried to climb into it. Second Officer Lightoller stopped them by waving his gun. The crew made a wall with their bodies while women and children got into the boat.

Now only two small lifeboats were left. Each boat could hold forty-seven people. They were still tied to a roof on the deck.

While the crew tried to free these last boats Captain Smith shouted to them, "Well, boys, do your best for the women and children!" Then he told them to save themselves.

There were still more than 1,500 people on the ship. Many of them looked for ways to survive. Others prepared to die.

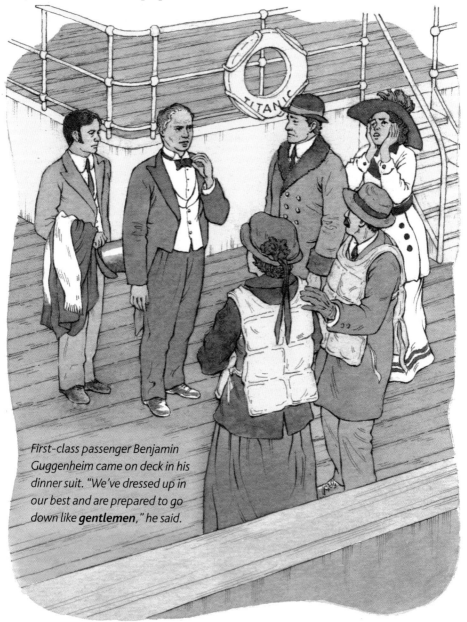

First-class passenger Benjamin Guggenheim came on deck in his dinner suit. "We've dressed up in our best and are prepared to go down like **gentlemen**," he said.

**gentleman** /ˈdʒɛntlmən/ (n) a polite man who acts well toward other people

At around 2:10 A.M., Wallace Hartley told the musicians in his band to save themselves. All eight musicians chose to stay with Hartley, and they played a final song together.

Suddenly, the front of the ship moved more quickly down into the water. A big wave began to move up the boat deck. The end was here.

## ● "It seemed a dream."

The deck was getting steeper and steeper. It was impossible to stand. There was a terrible crashing noise as furniture and plates fell. Many people were thrown into the water. Others jumped, hoping to swim to a lifeboat.

Radio operator Harold Bride was one of the men who was trying to free the last lifeboats. As the great wave came up the deck, one boat floated away on the water **upside-down**. More than twenty men climbed on top of it, but Bride was under the boat and he couldn't escape. For forty-five minutes, he held onto the boat in the freezing water.

In the great ship's final minutes, the lights went out. There was no moon that night, but some light came from the stars in the clear, dark sky. Suddenly, there was a new noise. This was the loudest of all and it could only mean one thing. The ship was breaking in two. People were still falling. Others chose to jump now. One passenger spoke of the last seconds as the ship sank:

*"Slowly . . . the water seemed to come up toward us . . . It seemed a dream."*

At 2:20 on the morning of April 15, the "Queen of the Ocean" was gone.

At first, the people in the lifeboats were most afraid for their own lives. One crewman shouted, "Pull for your lives." But they had to decide what to do. The *Titanic* was gone and hundreds of people were in the icy water of the North Atlantic. Some were holding onto furniture. Others were trying to swim. Many were screaming for help. To the people in the lifeboats, the noise seemed to fill the night.

upside-down /ˌʌpsaɪd ˈdaʊn/ (adv) with the top at the bottom and the bottom at the top

**A** As the front part of the ship sank, the back came up out of the water. It climbed higher and higher.

**B** The ship broke in two. The front part sank.

**C** The back part of the Titanic fell back. It sat flat in the water for a short time. Hope grew in some passengers. They probably thought, "It's going to float!"

**D** Then this part of the ship began to sink, too. Soon the back of the ship was high in the air. It didn't move for a few minutes. Then it began to sink, moving faster and faster into the dark water.

## 4.1 Were you right?

Look back at Activity 3.4. Then decide which sentence on the right follows each sentence on the left. Match them.

1  A boy tried to hide on a lifeboat.

2  The crew used a gun to keep back the crowds.

3  Benjamin Guggenheim put on his dinner suit.

4  Wallace Hartley was with his band.

a  They saved the lifeboats for women and children.

b  A crewman ordered him out of the boat.

c  The musicians all stayed for the final song.

d  He wanted to die like a "gentleman."

## 4.2 What more did you learn?

Look at the pictures of the *Titanic* sinking. Imagine that you were at the back of ship. Describe what happened there.

1 ..................................................
..................................................
..................................................

2 ..................................................
..................................................
..................................................

3 ..................................................
..................................................
..................................................

4 ..................................................
..................................................
..................................................

### .3 Language in use

Look at the sentences on the right. Then use these verbs to complete the sentences below.

| | | |
|---|---|---|
| climb | swim | get |
| play | prepare | scream |

> The *Titanic's* front end **was sinking** fast.
>
> The deck **was getting** steeper and steeper.

While the *Titanic* was sinking,

1 ... the crew .......................... the next lifeboat.

2 ... crowds .......................... into the lifeboats.

3 ... the water .......................... higher and higher on the deck.

4 ... the band .......................... .

5 ... people in the water .......................... for help.

6 ... many people .......................... toward the lifeboats.

### .4 What happens next?

Who do you think survived that terrible night? Check (✓) the names.

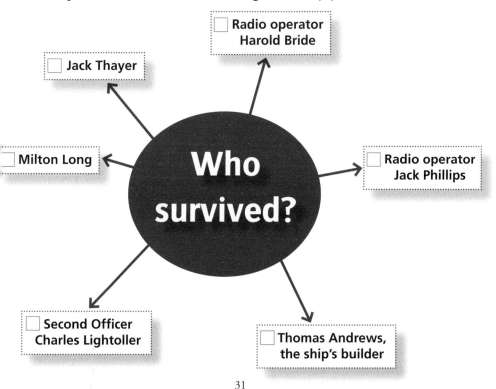

Radio operator Harold Bride

Jack Thayer

Milton Long

Who survived?

Radio operator Jack Phillips

Second Officer Charles Lightoller

Thomas Andrews, the ship's builder

# CHAPTER 4

# In the Water

*People in the boats waved and shouted. Some burned letters and papers so the* Carpathia *could see them.*

T he people in the lifeboats listened to all those cries for help. Imagine the terrible discussions.

You sit in the lifeboat. The cold is terrible. But you know that it is much, much worse for the people in the black water. You can hear their screams in the dark.

- "They can't stay alive in the freezing water," says a man in the boat. "It's too cold."
- "Our friends and relatives are dying!" shouts a woman holding a small child. "My husband stayed on the ship. We have to go back and help."

- The crewman shakes his head. "We can't. If we go back, too many people will try to get into the boat. Then, we'll all die."
- "We have to save ourselves now!" agrees a man at the back of the boat. He is crying as he speaks.

You listen in silence. The screams are becoming quieter, as the people in the water become weaker and weaker. Soon it will be too late.

What do you think? What was the right thing to do?

In fact, only one of the lifeboats did go back. Fifth Officer Harold Lowe ordered a search for survivors, but it was too late. When they arrived most people were dead. Only twelve people were pulled from the water.

One of the people in the water that night was young Jack Thayer.

# A Passenger's Story

## Part 3

Jack was a strong swimmer, but the water was icy.

I can't believe it. The ship is breaking in two!

Milton! Where are you?

But Jack never saw Milton Long again.

Most of the men on the boat were from the ship's crew.

Here, boy.

## ● The *Carpathia* arrives

When he received the *Titanic's* SOS message in the night, Captain Rostron of the *Carpathia* ordered his ship to go as fast as possible. There was a lot of ice in the area. But Rostron was a good captain. The *Carpathia* saw a rocket from one of the lifeboats at 4 A.M.—less than two hours after the *Titanic* sank.

It wasn't easy to find all of the survivors. The lifeboats covered a 6.5 kilometer (4-mile) area. It took Rostron and his crew four hours to pick up everybody. People in the boats waved and shouted. Some burned letters and papers so the *Carpathia* could see them.

Captain Rostron ordered his crew to count the survivors. They counted 705. Later, people guessed 711 or even 757 survivors. That meant that more than 1,500 of the *Titanic's* passengers and crew died.

## ● Who lived and who died?

- Bruce Ismay, the president of the White Star Line, escaped in one of the last lifeboats.
- Thomas Andrews, the ship's builder, died with the ship. He never even put his life jacket on.
- Captain Smith didn't survive. There was a newspaper story about him saving a baby in the water. It probably wasn't true.

- Harold Bride lived. He even worked in the radio room as the *Carpathia* sailed to New York.
- Jack Phillips wasn't as lucky as Bride. He swam to a lifeboat but died of cold in the night.
- Second Officer Charles Lightoller survived. He was the last survivor who climbed onto the *Carpathia*.
- Wallace Hartley and the musicians in his band went down with the ship.
- Molly Brown lived and became famous for her bravery on the night of the **disaster**. In 1960 there was even a musical play about her, *The Unsinkable Molly Brown*.
- Jack Thayer found his mother on the *Carpathia*. His father died on the *Titanic*. He later wrote a letter to Milton Long's parents, describing their son's last hours alive.

**FIRST CLASS**
*Men: 54 lived; 119 died.*
*Women and children: 145 lived; 10 women and 1 child died.*

**SECOND CLASS**
*Men: 15 lived; 142 died.*
*Women and children: 104 lived; 24 died.*

**THIRD CLASS**
*Men: 69 lived; 417 died.*
*Women and children: 105 lived; 119 died.*

**THE CREW**
*Men: 194 lived; 682 died.*
*Women: 20 lived; 3 died.*

## 5.1 Were you right?

Look at your answers to Activity 4.4. Then match these people with the sentences about them.

1 He was the last person to climb onto the *Carpathia*.

2 He survived but his father and his friend Milton Long did not.

3 He continued working on the *Carpathia*.

4 He left the ship in one of the last lifeboats.

5 He reached a lifeboat but later died of cold.

6 He died after—possibly—saving a baby.

a Bruce Ismay

b Captain Smith

c Radio operator Harold Bride

d Jack Thayer

e Radio operator Jack Phillips

f Second Officer Charles Lightoller

## 5.2 What more did you learn?

1 Imagine that you are one of the people in a lifeboat. Would you try to pick up more people from the water? Why (not)? Write reasons for and against.

Why?

Why not?

2 What were these people's hopes of surviving on the *Titanic*? Put them in order from 1 (the best hope) to 5 (least hope).

a men in third class ..............

b women and children in third class ..............

c men in the crew ..............

d women and children in second class ..............

e women and children in first class ..............

38

## 3 Language in use

Look at the sentences on the right. Then add a noun to the second sentences below so they have the same meaning as the first.

> Charles Lightoller **survived**.
>
> He was the last **survivor** who climbed onto the *Carpathia*.

1   The people in the lifeboats listened silently.

The people in the lifeboats listened in ...*silence*......... .

2   In the lifeboats, they discussed what to do.

There were .............................. in the lifeboats about what to do.

3   Many people were not as lucky as the survivors in the lifeboats.

Many people did not have as much .............................. as the survivors in the lifeboats.

4   The *Carpathia* searched for survivors for four hours.

The *Carpathia*'s .............................. for survivors lasted for four hours.

5   Molly Brown became famous because she was brave.

Molly Brown became famous for her .............................. .

## 4 What happens next?

Read the title of the next chapter and the lines in *italics* below it. Then discuss answers to these questions and make notes.

1   *Why did many people around the world not believe the news at first?*

2   *Why were people angry about the accident?*

3   *What happened to the survivors when they reached New York?*

# CHAPTER 5

# The World Cries

*Through newspapers and radio, the eyes of the world were on
the ship and its survivors.*

A t first, as the *Carpathia* traveled back to New York, no messages were sent to the waiting world. Some newspapers, still believing in the "unsinkable" ship, got the story completely wrong. In their news stories, the *Titanic* was safe and all the passengers were alive.

When the news was finally known, sadness and surprise were felt around the world. Ten thousand people were waiting when the *Carpathia* arrived in New York on the evening of Thursday, April 18. Through newspapers and radio, the eyes of the world were on the ship and its survivors.

Even after the terrible accident, things were very different for first-class and third-class passengers. The survivors from first-class were taken to the best hotels in New York. But the passengers from third-class were in a new country without any money or clothes, or any of their things.

Back in the North Atlantic, a ship was picking up dead bodies from the ocean. In the next six weeks, 328 bodies were found. The crew of the *Mackay-Bennet* didn't know who most of them were. But they did know John Jacob Astor IV, possibly the richest man in the world. He was carrying a big gold ring, a gold watch, and a lot of money when he died. None of it helped him.

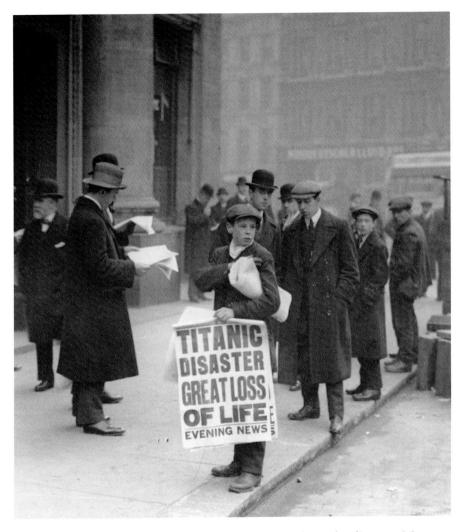

In Britain and the United States, people were angry about the **disaster**. Many questions were asked.

- Why didn't Captain Smith act on warnings about ice?
- Why did Bruce Ismay survive when his passengers died?
- Why didn't the *Californian* help when they saw rockets?
- Did a Norwegian fishing ship turn away from the *Titanic*?
- Why weren't there lifeboats for all the passengers?

disaster /dɪˈzæstə/ (n) something terrible that happens

41

## ● The Mystery Children

One of the strangest stories was the *Titanic's* mystery children. When the ship was going down, a man passed his two young sons into the last lifeboat. The father, "Louis Hoffman," didn't survive. The boys arrived in New York on the *Carpathia*. But nobody knew who they were. No family was found.

In fact, "Louis Hoffman" wasn't the father's real name. It was Michel Navratil. Navratil took the boys from their mother in France and decided to start a new life with them in the United States. He didn't want their mother to know. Finally, the mother saw her sons in a newspaper, and the boys were sent back to France. There they told her their father's last words: "Tell her that I loved her and still do."

## ● An Unbelievable Story

The Allisons were a rich family from Montreal in Canada, traveling in first class. An English nurse, Alice Cleaver, was looking after the family's two children, baby Trevor and his two-year-old sister Loraine.

On the night of the accident, the Allisons were on deck. Alice Cleaver picked up the baby. "I won't let him out of my arms," she told the boy's mother. Then she left and found a lifeboat. After she got to the *Carpathia*, she kept Trevor Allison with her. At the time, all the newspapers called her very brave. The rest of the Allison family were not so lucky: they died on the ship.

But the story of the Allison family and their nurse did not go away. In 1940, an American woman, Loraine Kramer, spoke on the radio. She was, she said, Loraine Allison! This was her story: Thomas Andrews, the ship's builder, carried her into one of the *Titanic's* lifeboats. She and Andrews lived together in the United States, and sometimes Bruce Ismay, the president of the White Star Line, visited them. He wanted them to hide because they knew secrets about the *Titanic*. It was an unbelievable story. Most people think that she was not Loraine Allison. She was probably looking for money.

Years later, the mystery about Alice Cleaver and the Allison family became even stranger. A book about the *Titanic* offered new information about the nurse that the Allisons did not know at the time. Cleaver, it said, was a killer—the murderer of her own child. Suddenly, there were lots of questions about Alice

Cleaver. Did she use baby Trevor to save herself? Years later, did she help Loraine Kramer with facts about the real Loraine Allison?

But the strange story of Alice Cleaver and the Allisons was not yet at an end. Historians found that there were two Alice Cleavers. A woman of this name *did* kill her own child in 1909, but she was not the woman on the *Titanic*. Now most people think that the Allisons' nurse did nothing wrong on that terrible night.

These stories showed that, years after the accident, people were still interested in the *Titanic*. The world saw one world war and then another, and the great ship lay in darkness at the bottom of the Atlantic. But many people dreamed of finding the *Titanic* again.

## ● "Leave it there."

The ocean was 4,000 meters (13,120 feet) deep where the *Titanic* lay. The water was black. Some people tried to find the ship, but without success.

In 1985, Robert Ballard and Jean Jarry were looking for the ship. There were twenty-three crew and twenty-three scientists on their ship, the *Knorr*. The team was using a submarine without a crew to search the bottom of the ocean. They worked for weeks and found nothing.

Then, on September 1, they saw pieces of metal on the ocean floor. Soon they couldn't believe what the camera was showing them. There was a big, dark shape in the water. It was the front part of the *Titanic*! The crew and scientists of the *Knorr* were silent for a minute, as they remembered the dead of the *Titanic*.

When the ship was discovered, some of the mysteries of the *Titanic* were solved:

- The front part of the ship lay 600 meters (1,970 feet) from the back. So the *Titanic* did break in two as it sank. Before the ship was discovered, people weren't sure about this.
- The ship sank 21 kilometers (13 miles) from the position that Jack Phillips and Harold Bride gave on the radio.

Ballard and his team returned the next year to look at more of the ship. All of the wood was gone, but some things on the ship looked almost new. Ballard's pictures of the *Titanic* became very famous. But Ballard didn't bring anything up from the *Titanic*. He wanted to leave it all at the bottom of the ocean.

In 1987, the ship was visited by a team with a different idea. This time the scientists went down in the submarine. They brought 1,800 things up from the *Titanic*. A box

from the ship was even opened
on a French TV show. It was
empty. Many of the survivors
were angry about all of this.
When Ballard was asked for
his opinion, he said, "In a
word, sad." This didn't stop the
French team returning a few
years later. They brought 3,600
things up from the *Titanic*.

What will the future of the
*Titanic* be? One business man
wants to sell trips to the ship. Will anyone ever bring the ship back up from the
bottom of the ocean? Survivor Eva Hart hoped not. Before her death in 1996,
she said, "Leave it there."

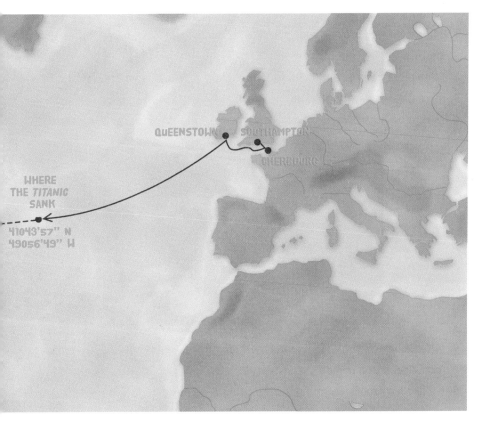

QUEENSTOWN    SOUTHAMPTON
CHERBOURG

WHERE
THE *TITANIC*
SANK

41043'57" N
49056'49" W

## 6.1 Were you right?

**Look back at Activity 5.4. Then decide if these sentences are true (✓) or untrue (✗)?**

1 ☐ At first some newspapers reported the *Titanic* story wrongly.
2 ☐ All survivors were taken to hotels in New York.
3 ☐ The third-class passengers were given new clothes and some money.
4 ☐ Many people were angry about the number of lifeboats on the ship.
5 ☐ People were angry because Bruce Ismay, the president of the White Star Line, died in the accident.

## 6.2 What more did you learn?

**Circle the correct information.**

1 Michel Navratil took his sons from France *without telling / to live with* their mother.
2 With his last words, Navratil sent a message of love to *his sons / his wife*.
3 Alice Cleaver was traveling on the *Titanic* with *her / another* family.
4 When the *Titanic* was sinking, Alice took *one child / both children* to a lifeboat.

5 After Robert Ballard's team found the *Titanic*, they *were silent / shouted with excitement* for a minute.
6 Ballard *left / took* everything that he found.

## .3 Language in use

Read the sentence on the right. Then complete the sentences below.

> The crew of the *Mackay-Bennet* didn't know **who** most of them **were**.

1 Everybody wanted to know
   <u>how many survivors there</u>
   <u>were</u>

> How many survivors are there?

2 Some people angrily asked
   ..............................................................
   ..............................................................

> Why is Bruce Ismay still alive?

3 Nobody knew
   ..............................................................
   ..............................................................

> Who are the Hoffman babies?

4 Many people weren't sure
   ..............................................................
   ..............................................................

> What should we think about Loraine Kramer's story?

5 The scientists wanted to know
   ..............................................................
   ..............................................................

> Where is the Titanic?

## 4 What happens next?

Look at the pictures in Chapter 6 from the movie *Titanic* and discuss Rose DeWitt Bukater and Jack Dawson. What kind of people are they in the movie? What happens to them on the ship? Make notes.

Notes

# The *Titanic* on Film

*James Cameron says that people always ask him about this.*
*Is Rose dreaming or is she dead? Cameron's answer? "You decide."*

When James Cameron was writing the movie *Titanic*, he wanted to show the rich history of the ship and its many true stories. He soon became sure of one thing. The love story between Rose and Jack was the most important part of the movie. If people worry about the two young lovers, they will understand the disaster more.

The movie's story doesn't begin in 1912. It starts in the present day, when Rose DeWitt Bukater is old. She thinks back to the past. The camera shows us the young Rose, when she sees the *Titanic* for the first time.

- British actress Kate Winslet played the young Rose, unhappy at the thought of her future with rich Cal Hockley (Billy Zane).
- All of the clothes here are exactly like the clothes of 1912.

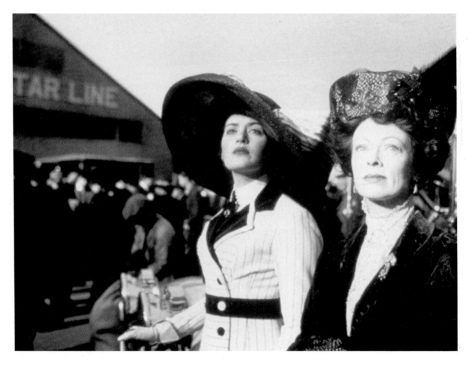

*Rose DeWitt Bukater is getting on the* Titanic *in Southampton. "It doesn't look any bigger than the* Mauritania*," she says, speaking about another famous ship.*

*Jack Dawson is a poor, young artist, traveling third class back to the United States from Europe.*

*First-class passengers listen while Jack Dawson explains his ideas about life. "Life's a gift," he says.*

- James Cameron later said about Leonardo DiCaprio, "I didn't want Leo at first." But after Leonardo read some lines, Cameron changed his mind. "I knew he was the guy."

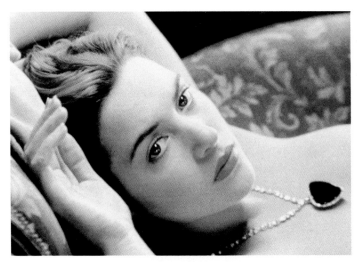

*Soon Rose and Jack fall in love. When Rose asks Jack to draw a picture of her, she is wearing nothing except "the Heart of the Ocean" around her neck.*

- This part of the movie was made on Leonardo DiCaprio's first day of filming. Important parts of a movie are often filmed at the beginning. The two actors later became good friends.

*The lookouts watch as Rose and Jack are together on the deck. When they look up, they will see the terrible shape of the iceberg in front of the ship.*

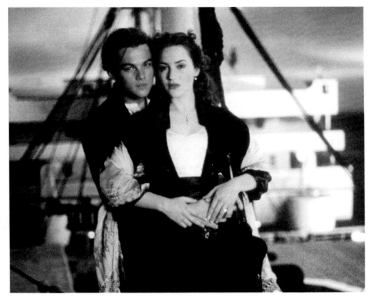

- Of course, this love story is a real difference between the movie and the real history of the *Titanic*. But, James Cameron explains, Rose's love for Jack plays a part in the terrible accident that follows.

*As the water comes higher and higher, Jack and Rose try to escape from Cal.*

- The actors in *Titanic* were often tired, wet, and cold. Later, DiCaprio described it as his hardest job.

*The crew send rockets high into the dark sky—but the* Titanic *is sinking.*

- In the 1958 movie *A Night to Remember*, the ship didn't break in two. Because of Ballard's work in 1985, Cameron and his team knew more about the ship's last seconds.

Jack Dawson, Rose DeWitt Bukater, and Cal Hockley weren't real people, but many of the people in the movie did exist.

The movie shows:
- Captain Smith and most of the ship's officers
- first-class passengers Molly Brown and Benjamin Guggenheim
- Bruce Ismay, the president of the White Star Line, and Thomas Andrews, the builder of the ship
- Jack Phillips and Harold Bride in the radio room

In the movie, Jack Dawson says that the cold water feels like "knives." These words come from one of the real survivors. Cameron read what many of the survivors wrote about *Titanic*. He used some of their words when he wrote

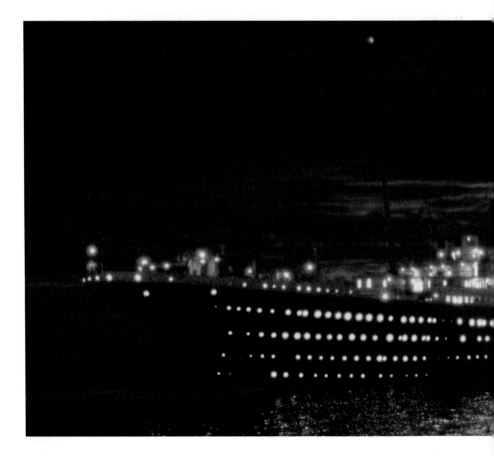

the movie. It was important to James Cameron to show these real people. He carefully planned the story so everything happened in the movie at exactly the right time. Try watching Cameron's movie again after reading this book. Can you see all of the things that are true?

But there are some mistakes in every movie. While Jack and Rose are walking on the deck, you can see a small hill with a building on it behind Jack. But they are in the middle of the Atlantic Ocean!

As Rose finishes her story to Brock Lovett and his crew, the last line of her story is, "He exists now only in my memory." Later, she throws the Heart of the Ocean into the Atlantic.

At the very end of the movie, we see Rose back on the *Titanic*. She is young again, and Jack Dawson is waiting for her. The two are together again. James Cameron says that people always ask him about this. Is Rose dreaming or is she dead? Cameron's answer? "You decide."

## ● "The world woke up ..."

After Cameron's movie, more and more people became interested in the story of the *Titanic*. Every year there are more and more books and videos on the subject.

But why? After so many years, why are people still interested in the *Titanic*? There have been worse accidents on the ocean in the years since then. What is so special about the *Titanic*?

◆

Some people think that the sinking of the *Titanic* showed the end of one part of history and the start of another. Before the *Titanic* sank, it was a time of great hope. People felt good about the world's future. Buildings were becoming taller, machines were becoming faster, and, of course, ships were becoming bigger and bigger. Anything seemed possible.

◆

For many people, that dream of a wonderful future sank with the *Titanic*. After April 15, 1912, the world seemed a different place. Just two years later, the First World War began. Millions of people died. New machines were used to kill more and more people.

◆

Maybe *Titanic* survivor Jack Thayer was right when he wrote, "The world woke up on April 15, 1912."

## 1 Why did the *Titanic* sink and so many people die?

a Look at the list below and write the numbers 0–5 next to the names. 0 means that those people had nothing to do with the accident. Write 5 if the actions of that person or group of people resulted, without question, in the deaths.

☐ the White Star Line ☐ the boat's builder

☐ Captain Smith ☐ the *Californian*

☐ the lookouts ☐ the Norwegian fishing ship

☐ the radio operators

b Discuss your list with another student and try to agree on your numbers.

## 2 The *Titanic* still lies at the bottom of the ocean. Should it stay there? Imagine that scientists now want to bring the ship up.

a Do you think this is a good idea? Or do you agree with *Titanic* survivor Eva Hart? Make notes for and against.

Notes

Bring the *Titanic* up!

Leave it there!

b Have a class discussion. Then have a vote.

**Read again the story of Jack Thayer, "A Passenger's Story." Then imagine that you are Jack Thayer. Write a diary page about one day of your trip on the *Titanic*, or about a day in your life immediately after the disaster.**

*1912*

Jack Thayer

**1** **Work in pairs. Find out more about life in the year 1912, the year when the *Titanic* sank. Use a library or the Internet.**

   **a**  Add information to these ideas.

   **b**  Make a poster for the classroom wall. Show what you learned about 1912.

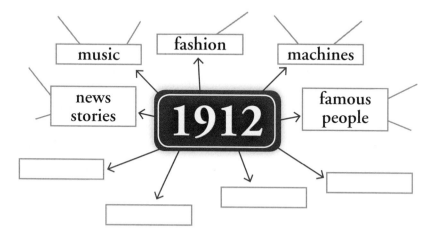

**2** **Interviews are important before memories are lost.**

   **a**  Make notes to prepare for this interview.

**Student A**   You are a passenger who survived the accident. Decide what happened to you. Which class were you in on the ship? Did you get into a lifeboat or did you jump into the water? What happened when you reached New York?

**Student B**   You are a radio news reporter in New York. Prepare questions for a *Titanic* survivor. What happened on the ship? How does he/she feel about the accident now? Has his/her life changed as a result?

Notes

   **b**  Have the interview. If possible, record it and play it for other students.

**Work in small groups and find out about an important day in the history of the world, or of your country.**

a Choose an important day in the last seventy years. Here are some ideas:
  • the end of the Second World War, 1945
  • the fall of the Berlin Wall, 1989
  • the attack on the World Trade Center in New York, 2001

b Use a library or the Internet to find out more about this day. Make notes.

Notes

c Decide how you are going to present this information to other students, and prepare your presentation. You can, for example:
  • write a newspaper report
  • make a poster
  • make a news program for radio or television and record it
  • give a short talk.

**4** **Interview somebody about your day in history.**

   **a** Find a person who remembers that day well. The person must speak English! Prepare a list of questions.

   **b** Ask your questions and record the answers. Remember that a good interviewer is a good listener. Ask more questions about the most interesting parts. Sometimes the best question is not on your list!

Interview Questions

Where were you when you heard the news?

**5** **Make a "Library of Living History."**

   **a** Decide, as a class, how you can best present to other people the information from Activity 4.

     • Will you have a "living history library" with tapes of the interviews that other students can borrow? Will you write notes to explain more about the interviews?

     • Will you have a "Library of Living History Day," when groups play their interviews?

     • Will you put the interviews on a history Web site for other people to play?

   **b** Make your "Library of Living History."